Goal Setting for Personal Success

The 7 Steps Guide to Achieve Everything You Want in Your Life, the Principles of a Successful Mindset for Change Your Habits and Your Results

Stephen Charles Clear

I

circumstances will any legal responsibility or blame be held against the publisher for any reparation, damages, or monetary loss due to the information herein, either directly or indirectly.

Respective authors own all copyrights not held by the publisher.

The information herein is offered for informational purposes solely, and is universal as so. The presentation of the information is without contract or any type of guarantee assurance.

The trademarks that are used are without any consent, and the publication of the trademark is without permission or backing by the trademark owner. All trademarks and brands within this book are for clarifying purposes only and are the owned by the owners themselves, not affiliated with this document

Introduction

Hello, dear reader. How often do you set goals, and do you finish what you started? Do you know exactly what you want from the future and what kind of person you want to become? Most people do not know. They were lazy or just did not think about it. So what kind of person do you want to become in 5 years? Just take a piece of paper and write down your plans for the future - this already increases the chances of becoming much better. This training book is dedicated to the professional setting and achievement of goals. Unfortunately, a critical attitude towards learning is found all over the world. Even in places like Europe and America, such is the case. In the East, education takes place in this way: while a person is studying, he absorbs everything that his mentor says.

This training is for those who are ready to learn, absorb new information. And put everything into practice - of course, while getting results. Very often when performing tasks people try to do things their own way. To get a good result, let's temporarily refuse to act in this way. Tasks will be complicated each time. The human psyche is very inert, and at first, it may seem to you that the training is not too complicated. In order to accelerate, it will be necessary to move from performing light actions to more complex ones, gradually increasing the load. We will act as in sports: professional weightlifters, coming to training after a long break, do not undertake to immediately pull the maximum weight. They start small, and then every day increases the load. The results that they achieve in this way are much better than if they came and immediately grabbed a huge barbell.

A goal is a long-term achievement. Usually, they focus on what you want to achieve in the future. It is important to set goals as they give you direction. Here are a few of the benefits of setting personal goals. Setting a goal helps you move forward, reminding you of an achievement that needs to be completed within a few days. Recording a goal provides an external idea of inner desire and becomes a constant reminder of what needs to be done. Usually, the goal is to excite you and create motivation for more hard work. Setting a goal allows you to focus on it, and frequent visualization helps to improve communication with desires. Communication is enough motivation to work even in difficult times because it becomes part of you. Some tasks seem too big, and you begin to doubt your ability to achieve. Setting goals can help you prevent frustration because it breaks down big frightening things into smaller plans that you can achieve gradually. Planning for smaller goals, which lead to achieving more, simplifies the formulation of an action plan that you begin to implement in the right way from the very beginning. Studies show that smaller stages provide real motivation and greater satisfaction.

You will be more responsible for achievements and failures, simply setting goals. Recording specific goals with a timetable for achieving results allows you to evaluate your achievements. You can always look back and overestimate the method you used if it crashes. This opens your eyes to what you have been doing for months or years. You will quickly determine if you have reached your goal and the changes that need to be made to the implementation plan if you have not reached the target point at that time.

Setting a personal goal makes you live a meaningful life because you cannot achieve much without a plan. You have to work on it. Setting a personal goal will benefit you by deciding what you need to do, and the deadlines are running out. Many coaching and self-help programs take the axiom that goal setting is a key factor in achieving success. Is it so? And is it really that setting a direction vector can always lead us to a positive result? Surprised by the question? Well, for the realization of the purpose of life, a person has enough average abilities, but not enough average courage. The strength of the mind needs a push to resist the circumstances and prejudices of others and push ahead. No better way to do that than by, of course, knowing first of all what you would like to achieve. I promise to show you all of these in this book.

Why set goals? Our ambitions are fuel, and talents are resources to overcome obstacles, but they mean nothing if we do not move purposefully. The result is important, while the winners are not judged, but "the tree that does not bear fruit is cut down." While you can ignore the desire for results and meditate on focusing on the process, but these are your troubles. The world appreciates only what you are capable of creating. The world pays for the result. Therefore, the ability to set and achieve a goal is more important than ambition and talent. For 100 people who have achieved success, 100% falls on those who were able to move purposefully, and 0% of those who were ambitious and talented, but were not able to move purposefully. The question is not your passion and power, but the ability to focus your energy. To move purposefully, you need a strategic direction, a goal in the short run and the ability to focus.

When there is no direction and goals, there is no way to build priorities. Since there is no way to build priorities, it is impossible to plan, because you can never manage your only resource - time. When you do not have goals and direction, it is impossible to focus. If there is no focus, then you cannot aim and shoot, because you do not know where. The answer is simple - create goals.

Are you ready? Then let's get started!

Chapter **1**

The First Step:
Mission Impossible!

Setting Goals and Dealing with Distractions

Let's complete the first task - for this, you will need a piece of paper with a pen. You need to write five "tails" - tasks that you never did. What is meant by tails? Maybe you forgot to give someone else's book or didn't call someone. Maybe you have long had to do something around the house. Write the tails that hang on you for a long time.

In this task, we will learn how to perform the most important stage in achieving goals - action. Think about it; maybe your faucet is flowing at home or you forgot to repay the debt. Maybe your baseboard is torn off or the ceiling is not painted. If there are many trails, choose the five most unpleasant. Next, you need to do the following: you need to write out five actions that will improve your health. Then record on paper five actions that will improve your business. Next, there are five actions that will improve your personal life and relationships with your family. And finally, five actions that you love to do and that bring you pleasure.

If we talk about health, then surely you want to look beautiful, charming, and athletic. Write five specific actions to help improve your health. Maybe it's a morning run or some kind of exercise. The same goes for business. Those who do business know what actions need to be done to improve it. The same applies to your personal life and your family and what you like to do most of all, which brings you pleasure and vivid impressions, but which, most likely, you do not.

Next, you should select one action from each category. Take your list and circle what you think is the most unpleasant, or what you want to do the most. So, from each sphere you have chosen one action - this is what you need to implement in the first place. During the execution of this task, try to track as much as possible all the components that were disclosed above. This is desire, choice and concrete action. The result of the exercise should be at the end of the completed action. For example, if in the category "health" the main item you chose to jog tomorrow morning, then tomorrow you really need to get up and run.

Achieving goals and training this skill in yourself may not be a particularly popular topic. But this is very important; without this, you cannot become a truly successful person.

Where Do People Get Their Energy From, What Sources of It Exist?

For most people, this is food, positive emotions, sports, and/or the desire to actively act. These options are not bad. And which emotion is one of the strongest for most people? This is fear - and this is one of the most powerful sources of energy.

Imagine a case that actually occurred in Russia. A man fell off the balcony and sagged over it with his arms for two hours until the EMERCOM officers arrived and took him off. And then this same man tried to hang on a horizontal bar after the incident and could barely hold out for seven minutes. Fear is a very powerful source of energy. Unfortunately, this is almost the only way to make people move at least somehow. If you look at others, you can see an interesting category - human-vegetable. These are people who have no goals, who especially do not achieve anything; they do not need anything. They simply exist; they have food, sleep, and probably occasionally some outbursts of emotions. And it's all. They do not require anything from life; they live for themselves.

If you are engaged in business and you have experience in managing people, remember: what best motivates employees to work? The first option: "Listen, staff, you and I will set a goal for three months. If you do a certain amount of work every day during this period, in the end, we will encourage you. You will get good money." This is the first way to motivate.

The second way is this: every day you stand behind the staff with a whip and, if he doesn't do something, you beat him with that whip. A whip can serve as fines, reprimands, or some other punishment. What method is more effective - to show a carrot somewhere in the distance or to stand behind a man with a whip all the time? Unfortunately, the second method is more effective. For most people, the avoidance strategy works much better. They have energy when someone kicks them from behind. They understand that if they do not work, they will not receive a salary or they will be fired. In general, there is always some fear. But this method is not for those who are set to achieve truly serious goals. This energy source helps to avoid something but is unlikely to achieve significant results in achieving the goal. The second very powerful source of energy is the achievement of goals. When you set a goal and achieve it, several factors play a role here, which give you energy.

Firstly, this is the goal itself. You clearly see her, visualize. You can feel how it will be when you reach it. Due to the fact that you imagine this feeling, you really want to experience it in reality. Athletes who are preparing for a competition always imagine how they will win the competition, how they will become winners. They scroll in their heads as they make a decisive jerk, throw, or blow. There is a continuous process of visualization. Since they constantly represent this, they are so merged with their goal that the body itself pulls them to come to victory. This method of scooping energy from goals is not available to most people around you. At the same time, it can help you really take off enormously.

Another source of energy is that when you repeatedly achieve goals, even small ones, it increases your self-confidence. You have tremendous powers because you understand that you can really set goals and achieve them. For most people, it works like this: set a goal, and then it did not work out. "Well, it didn't work out. Well, I couldn't ..." ... and that's it. Next time the attitude will be the same. A person sets himself some goal, and in case of failure he thinks: "It didn't work, so it didn't work." In such a situation, there is no source of energy, since everything is done passively enough.

In order for the goals to truly serve as a source of tremendous energy for you, you need to take into account and observe one very important nuance that few people understand. Unfortunately, the goals set in the head do not work. One of the features of our brain is that what we hold in our heads is very poorly fixed. The head is an excellent generator of ideas, but you should not constantly keep goals in mind, especially if there are a lot of them. At the same time, we are able to control about five processes. Developed people - seven processes. Since everyday life constantly throws up a bunch of problems for us, this resource is wasted on small current affairs. For serious aspirations, there simply is no place left in the head. Even if you think that you keep the goal in your memory, in fact, you may already have forgotten to think about it. Therefore, it is imperative to transfer your goals to paper, electronic media, and so on. If we talk about material things, then we mean a car, a house, travel, and the like. So, these goals that we set are not really our goals. These are the aspirations that are imposed on us.

All media - television, newspapers, and magazines - have one single goal: to sell as much product as possible. More precisely, they provide advertising, and the task of advertising is just to sell. Gigantic funds are being invested in the media in order to instill certain values into the overwhelming mass of the population. For example, it is important to drive a car of just such and such a class. Or take the phones. Surely there is a person in your environment who is constantly changing mobile phones. He seems to have just bought a new one, and here came even a more advanced model. And although the old phone is only six months old and it works very well, it's morally outdated. How can one live with it further? This is not just happening, it is the systematic work of the media and marketers. Their task is to make us constantly buy. Take a look around at the ads that surround us on the roads, at bus stops, in magazines. In fact, she shouts to us one word: "Buy!" A consumption model is being built into us and very often this model has little in common with our true goals, with what we really want.

Surely you are familiar with this situation - you have long wanted to buy a thing. And here you have the opportunity. The first month usually passes in a certain euphoria, and then everything becomes completely natural and does not bring any joy. Let's say a TV with a huge diagonal - that's cool! And then it turns out that this is cool only the first time, and then nothing, completely neutral. This is one example of achieving goals that are not entirely yours. When you achieve your true goals, it constantly brings you joy, gives energy and strength. If you really want something, you can test your goal by renting a wish object. This way you will understand if this is really what you need. Otherwise, then it is very disappointing when the thing quickly ceases to bring the proper emotions.

Here, say, one person has long dreamed of a yacht. As a result, he bought it, and it turned out the following - it is very expensive to service it. He only gets to go on a yacht for two to three weeks a year, and the rest of the time it is idle and brings only a headache. It is necessary to monitor it, clean the bottom, a whole bunch of problems arise. And now this man is suffering, thinking that it would be better to rent a yacht. For many purposes, the same thing can happen to you, so I highly recommend that you first try them out. If there is a global goal, for example: "I want a villa somewhere on the coast of France!" Try renting it for a month. Save up money, rent a villa and see how it feels. It may well turn out that you don't need it at all and it's much easier to take it off. This applies mainly to large goals.

Exercises

Now let's do the exercise. Draw a table with five vertical columns. Each of these columns is a fragment of your life. Select the steps at your discretion, as it will be convenient for you. For example - a day nursery, kindergarten, school, institute, work. That is, you need to note the main large fragments when your life has seriously changed. Here we go to kindergarten, no worries. Then the school - here everyday life is completely different. This is due to the emergence of a certain responsibility, for example, for homework. Then something new happens at the institute, and so on until today.

Describe how this happened and is happening with you, divide the past and present by turning points in terms of your daily life. You can write a stage before school when you lived with your parents and you especially did not have to do anything, then elementary school, high school. The main thing is to do it for yourself, as you prefer. Now you need to remember each of these segments. It is necessary to recall in memory the most vivid actions and events that occurred at each stage. Remember what you liked most to do in this period of life, which left the most vivid impressions. For each period, try to recall at least a few points. Enter them in the appropriate column.

It is not necessary to describe in detail all the events. It is important that you yourself understand and can remember them. Let's say the record is "volleyball" - and you understand that you really enjoyed playing volleyball. Maybe it was a camping trip. Or some major change in life happened. For women, for example, is the birth of a child. The most interesting observation is this: unhappy people are those who simply stop doing what used to bring them happiness. Your task is to find those events, things that brought you real joy, which you could do for days on end and feel like the happiest person. Once you find it, start putting it into practice.

Tasks

1. Write the five most unpleasant tails that hang on you.
2. Write five actions that will help improve your health.
3. Write five steps to help improve your business or career.
4. Write five actions that will help improve relationships in your personal life and in communicating with your family.
5. Write down the five things you love to do most that bring you joy and pleasure.
6. Select one action from each category and complete it tomorrow.
7. Divide life into five segments (maybe more) and in each write what you liked to do the most.

Chapter **2**

The Second Step:
Perpetual Motion

Many people begin to compare themselves with those who are already several levels higher. For example, if you are in business, then starting to compare yourself with Richard Branson or Donald Trump, saying: "They earn a million times more money than me, and what should I do now?" - This is not very correct. It pretty demotivates. Today you earn $1,000, tomorrow you earn 2,000, the day after tomorrow 3,000, but compared to Trump's annual income, it's all the same little things.

The correct approach is different: every day you need to compare yourself with yourself yesterday. When you see that every day you make small, but a step forward, become a little better than yesterday, then you can achieve your goals correctly. Of course, you need to look at other people, but do not compare yourself with them; otherwise, it will strongly demotivate you. You will always find those who are several steps above you. And if you constantly think, what a loser you are in comparison with them, this will not have a positive impact.

Very often, setting goals, people tend to get away from something. For example: "I want my life not to have this!" - So that I don't have to work for my uncle, that I don't have to do what I don't like, and so on. If you set yourself the goal of never feeling a lack of money, getting out of poverty is a bad goal. You need to strive for something and not run away from something. If you are trying to run away from something, then, of course, you will come somewhere, but this "somewhere" may turn out to be far from the place you would really like to get into.

Regarding financial goals. Often a person sets himself the goal: "I want to make a million dollars!" If we are talking about finances, it is much better to set ourselves the goal of having some kind of cash flow that will go on all the time. Permanent income is more important. Break a big jackpot, win, earn a lot of money - all this is good. But it is much more important that you have just a constant flow. Therefore, when you set yourself any financial goals, then, first of all, plan what income you will have. Do not earn some kind of a lot of money, namely a constant stable income. It can be a passive income.

Is Discussing Your Plans a Great Idea?

The next mistake is that often we are afraid to set ambitious goals. Especially if we tell someone about this, we say: "I want to achieve such a goal, I want to travel four to five months a year." As soon as you voice it (especially if you say it to your relatives and friends), you immediately have a bunch of sworn friends who will rush to stop you. They will be happy to explain to you why you will never succeed. They will also tell you why this absolutely certainly does not need to be done, why it is bad, dangerous — they will put you in "prison," "shoot" you for it, and you will be deeply unhappy.

Surely you met the following: as soon as you set yourself an interesting goal, a stream of negativity suddenly began to pour from you. They told you that you won't succeed, that you don't have to do this, and that this is a stupid occupation. Unfortunately, this is common and usually comes from close relatives. In fact, the reason here is as follows. When you set a seriously ambitious goal (and God forbid, you achieve it), people around you do not like it, because your success is very hard on their pride. Immerse yourself a little in the psychology of people. There you are and there are some of your friends. Now you are at about the same social level - in terms of income, in how you relax, have fun, work. Suppose you decide to start working hard, to work better. Maybe you dare to open your own business.

When you tell your friends about this, they have an alternative - to start doing something too, and for this, you need to tear your ass off the couch and strain, which you really do not want. The second option is to do nothing, and then you will have to find an excuse for this. Naturally, they find an excuse by deciding that nothing will work, that it makes no sense and there is no need to waste time. Then the following happens. You achieve the serious work planned after two or three years. It turns out that you earn substantially more money, that in comparison with those around you go to relax in more interesting and exotic places. And you live in a better place. The difference becomes noticeable.

Thus, when you start to rise, then from your acquaintances, relatives, friends, you knock out the very excuse from under your feet. Because you were at the same level as they, and, having reached a new level, you actually proved that they could do the same. Let now reap the fruits of their own idleness - they themselves chose to sit on the couch and do nothing. You show in practice - they themselves are to blame for being significantly lower than you. This very strongly affects people's pride. Previously, they had an excuse, but here you do not leave an excuse. Since such situations have occurred with most people, they subconsciously begin to react in a certain way. As soon as you try to take off, to realize some new ideas in any field - be it career, business, personal life, sport, health - they immediately try to drive you back. This is because if God forbid, you succeed, then they will no longer have excuses - why they are lower than you. This is unpleasant and a little cynical, but, unfortunately, it is. Therefore, when you want to start something, then take it and do it without telling anyone.

Most people will always come up with a lot of excuses for not doing something. But if you have already begun to act, then they will not dare to hinder you. Therefore, set the goals that you really want to achieve. If failure suddenly overtook you, say: "Well, well done, you were right; it didn't work out." But more often, you will succeed.

Exercises

Let's get back to our exercises. How much have you been able to analyze your life since childhood? Did you manage to remember the things that you liked to do? How well were the early years recalled in general? How many pleasant moments came to mind or did you have a difficult childhood with toys nailed to the floor? If I recall a lot, then this is excellent. It is very good if you get a lot of points in each of the blocks. Look at your notes and try to combine similar bright moments into blocks by categories. For example, you see that at different times in your life you enjoyed learning foreign languages. Maybe you loved meeting friends; maybe you enjoyed doing some sports.

Go through the whole chain: school, institute, work and find similar bright moments. Now combine them and write them out separately. What you have highlighted are your values. It really matters to you; it is these actions that give you energy. You need to continue to do these things. If you are not already doing them now, then start introducing them into your life. Not necessarily in the same form, maybe a little different. In childhood, for example, you liked to learn languages, then you enjoyed doing it at school, at college. If you begin to actively speak to them now, it will also give you pleasure. If you liked to practice some kind of sport - similarly. If you liked to manage people - excellent, most likely, you continue to do this. These values are what you need to build your life around. When you start writing down your goals, be sure to include these values in them so that they always take place in your life.

These are the very values, the very goals, the achievement of which will bring you tremendous energy. Moreover, this energy will not be one-off. For example, if you set yourself the goal of buying a car of a different brand, then most likely it will bring you energy, but only for a while. A month, a half month, two, then it will become routine. But if you find and reveal your true values, bring them into your life, then from here, you will constantly draw energy. This is such an inexhaustible source that must be used. So look at your list, highlight similar bright moments in it and write them into categories. When you work on goals, you will at least not forget about these things. Be sure to embed your values in goals - both in the near and long-term.

Patterning Your Goals

Goals should be related to early hobbies directly or indirectly. For example, you liked to learn languages, and now you are going to travel to a country whose language you once studied. This is precisely the indirect intersection, which will affect you very positively. If you remember that you have always been a leader - the headman in the classroom, at the university - then you are clearly pleased to manage people. You like to be the main thing- to be in sight. You should also bring this into your life, that is, advance to leadership positions or engage in management. These values must be sought. The older we get, the deeper they hide, because in most cases we do not work on them. But if we take them to the light, they bring a lot of pleasure and positive energy.

Earlier, you got the task: to identify five specific actions from several categories that will help improve any area of your life. And today it is necessary to complete one action to achieve this goal. This task was given in order for you to accelerate, because, I repeat, the human psyche is quite inert. If you have not completed the task to the end, we recommend that you complete it and, if possible, do it today. If you accumulate outstanding tasks, then to do them all at once later simply will not work. The load will gradually increase. The development of goals is very serious work, which must be treated accordingly.

Earlier, we talked about the fact that our brain is designed in such a way that it cannot perform more than five to seven tasks at a time. Therefore, it is very important not to keep goals in mind - they should be written out. The fact is that about sixty thousand thoughts arise daily in a person's head. Scientists have proven that 95% of these thoughts are repeated. If for the most part you think about the series that are shown on television, about what is happening in the world, especially about the negative news, then more negative things appear in your life. If you pay more attention to your goals, think about what you want to achieve, then you come to your goals and to your dreams. This is very important to understand.

Do Goals Need to Be Written Out?

Quite frankly, yes. The fact is that when you do this, you pick out from among the sixty thousand thoughts and mark with red flags exactly those that relate to your goals - what you really want to achieve. Such flags are set in your brain, and you begin to think in exactly the way in which you need to think in order to achieve goals. It's better not to work on a computer, but on paper: when you write, it affects the brain and consciousness very much.

Opportunities That Help Achieve Goals

Once you begin to set goals, decide what you want to achieve, suddenly, out of nowhere, new opportunities appear. New people appear with whom you begin to cooperate, some new things, directions appear. Understand the most important thing - you need to be prepared for change. At first, they may not seem very good to you, not very positive. Let's imagine a man who wants to improve his life. He sets himself specific goals, for example: "I want to get an income of 10 thousand dollars a month. I want to be a person who is respected, appreciated and listened to by other people," and so on.

Imagine a certain fellow who works every day and sets himself the goal of improving his life. What can happen? For example, he is fired from his job. What do most people think when this happens in their lives? They decide that the world is unfair to them. Where are the incomes that they dreamed about, where is the salary increase? People begin to blame heaven (or the boss, or the government) for everything, that everything turns out unfairly. If we alienate this situation a bit and look at it all from above, we will see the following picture. A man dreamed of starting to live a better life, and life itself begins to slip various possibilities to him. Dismissal from work, I think, is a very good chance to start something of your own. It is possible to open your own business or finally do what a person wants to do, from which he enjoys.

Difficult Situations Must Be Considered from the Perspective of Opportunities

When you set goals (especially if they are ambitious and make you tremble), when you just think about them, then in life certain changes immediately begin. You need to be prepared for them and understand that the changes that arise in your life just lead you to the goals that you set for yourself. Let's move on to the assignments. The next thing to do: from the list of five actions in a variety of areas, you need to select one item and execute it. Further, the task is a little more complicated: look a little ahead and write down the goals that you want to achieve in your life. You should imagine what you want to achieve in your entire life.

Think about the answers to the questions:

1. What do I want to achieve?
2. What do I want to have?
3. What kind of person do I see myself as? (This refers to how you look, what you do.)
4. How much money do I want to receive?

This exercise is quite difficult and requires a certain amount of time. We recommend that you retire and try to get in touch with what you want to get from your life. This is very important to do, because further you will have a stronger task, and the present will serve as a good preparation for it. As for the term, let's say the following. You write goals for life. Fix everything that comes to mind. Do not set specific dates; this can be done later. Now just think about what you want to achieve. No need to put any financial restrictions. All the restrictions are in your head. Reflect on goals from each category. Do not develop in one direction; think about what you want to achieve in each area.

Tasks

1. Define your values.

2. Select one action out of every five categories recorded from chapter 1 and do it tomorrow. In the report, write off what exactly was done.

3. Write your goals. How do you see your life? What do you want to achieve? What to have? How to look? What to do? What income stream to have? Try to do it as detailed as possible.

Chapter **3**

The Third Step:
Resource State

Want to achieve your goals? Then you just need strong intrinsic motivation. This is fuel for your achievements. Just as a car cannot drive without gas, you are not moving towards goals without energy. Therefore, over the next two days, we will actively increase internal energy and develop motivation.

Intrinsic Motivation

Information in itself does not change life. Life changes for the better with motivation. What it is? This is directly related to energy. Simply put, motivation is internal energy- the intention to do something. You not just want something, but turn on, take it and start to do something in order to achieve your goal. Motivation is your inner strength. This is a high level of energy, internal resources - physical, emotional, psychological. It is much more difficult to achieve your goal without internal fuel, and you simply will not be able to achieve some goals due to a lack of strength.

As we have said, motivation is energy, drive, intent. It represents an irresistible desire to do something, to achieve something, and this desire is transformed into action. Motivation leads to the transformation of your intentions and desires into actions. It serves as a kind of base, without which nothing works. For example, self-discipline without motivation does not work. You can structure yourself indefinitely, write plans, force yourself to do something, but so far there is no motivation - the process is very difficult. How is motivation different from willpower? Could you force yourself to do something from under a stick? If you have an intrinsic motivation, an intention to take and do, then you simply do, and there is no violence against yourself.

For example, when you want to eat, get up and go for food. And you don't have to force yourself to walk eighteen steps to the refrigerator, open the door with your will and take out the sausage. Everything happens naturally because there is motivation. When you are engaged in self-development - whether you are increasing your income, building relationships, developing a business or just want to harmonize your life, then you go through a process of some growth. In special cases, the process of developing a business, developing relationships, but the most important thing is the process of developing yourself. It all starts with yourself!

Remaining the same person, it is impossible to achieve new results. It is necessary to take new actions, think differently, communicate with other people - and, accordingly, become a different person. This is the only way to self-development and success.

Procrastination

At what point is growth a shift in the direction of development? Are you familiar with postponing cases for later? Surely this happened to you: it seems like there is a goal, and you want to do something, but still, you put it off and put it off. Therefore, you get mediocre results. This situation is annoying from time to time because you seem to know and know everything, but for some reason, you are not doing anything. Surely you would like in such cases to gain access to energy, to be able to get involved in achieving a goal, at work.

So, at what moment does the same click, shift occur, when you suddenly begin to act actively? For some reason, you stop being distracted, work, forget about all social networks, do not watch TV - all this happens naturally. Why is this happening? Try to answer this question yourself first. Speak a few options out loud or write them down. Click, that very switch occurs in two cases. The first option is when you have a crisis. For example, you have been fired from work, and a loan is hanging on you, from which there is no escape. Now you simply have to make money, regardless of your desire or unwillingness to do it. A crisis has occurred, and you simply have no other choice. Crisis situations can be associated not only with monetary issues. It can be any situation in life when everything is twisted into a too-tight knot and it is simply impossible to continue to sit still. In this case, you begin to move and act. This is a pain option.

The second shift option is a strong inspiration. For example, you have long wanted to change a car, but it is too difficult from a financial point of view, and there is no time, and you put up with the situation. One fine day, you accidentally get into a friend's car, and he gives you a chance to drive it, and in his car, there's not one hundred horsepower, but four hundred! You press the pedal to the floor and understand that this is a real drive; this is unrealistically cool! After that, you transfer to your car, and you don't like it anymore. You are now a fan; you're hooked on something. It may not necessarily be a car; it may be a sport, a hobby, a job — anything. You become a fan. You understand that further life without an object of adoration is simply impossible. And you no longer have the option to go back - the fire of desire is burning within you. You tried it; it became your passion; you need it like air and water.

Did crises happen to you when you began to act actively? There were moments, outbursts of passion when you also developed a vibrant activity in the direction of achieving the goal? You come home and understand that just sitting and doing nothing is no longer possible. This condition must be used! The options described above - pain and pleasure - are classic. Crisis and passion are two sides of the same coin, two poles of the same scale. For example, when you exercise in the gym, you do ten repetitions. Which of these repetitions creates 80% muscle growth? The correct answer is twelfth. Not the tenth, not the ninth, but the twelfth. And what kind of repetition creates 90% growth, to which score does a good coach finish you? The correct answer is the fourteenth repetition. Now we are talking about a situation where ten is the limit for you, you can no longer. So it is precisely when you can no longer - you must do it!

If You Can't, You Must!

Remember this phrase. Its meaning is that if you can no longer do something, you can no longer lift this bar, take it and do it a couple more times. This will make you a winner. The conversation is not only about the gym, but it also applies to any activity. You have been working today for eighteen hours; your eyes are sticking together, fall off your feet ... Work for another hour, create an additional result. Extra minutes, hours, those repetitions that seem already unrealistic - they create the result and separate successful people from everyone else. You must become such people - winners.

Cross the line - this is what creates growth and important changes. It is necessary to constantly work on yourself, learn to go beyond your usual capabilities. This will help to grow and achieve completely new results, to reach a new level of development. Overcoming, crisis, craving or meaning that you create in your activity - this is exactly what switches you from a passive state to an active one. This is a lever for growth. There is another important key that helps to switch from a state where you know everything and can, but do nothing, into a state of active activity, when a lot of energy appears. We spoke about the first levers - this is a crisis and a passionate desire to go beyond the limits of possibilities.

Now let's talk about the second important resource. In order for the transition to action to take place, you need energy. If there is no energy and strength, then on one moral motivation you will not go far. Energy is in a peak state; this is the second key to action. The internal peak state is when you are active and charged. Remember the situation from your life when you were on a horse. As if megawatts of energy have been pumped into you, and you are ready to ride day and night. Imagine this state now - you hear, see, feel the same as then. Create a picture of such a situation before your eyes. Each of you in your life had many such conditions when you were really turned on. Perhaps this was a little different than described above. Restore this state, fix it, "anchor."

Anchoring

Anchoring is as follows. You connect the necessary internal state with some action, with certain music, with a keyword. For example, you jump to the music, raise your hands up and shout: "Know." It turns out a kind of ritual, a whole set of anchors that work altogether. You can choose something completely different, something your own.

Let's create one anchor. Once you understand the principle, you can create many more for yourself. For this, you will need music. Stand up, push the chair away. Now straighten your back, straighten your shoulders, and you cannot just straighten them, but stretch them a little. Move your hands, bend to one side, the other, back, forward, and shake. Further to the music, remember the peak state in which you were unrealistically cool. As soon as you hear music, start moving, jumping, and be sure to smile. Straighten your back, shoulders and jump in place. You can close your eyes. Remember the state when you were very healthy when you felt an energy boost.

Keep moving and smile, remember - what did you see then? Imagine this picture before your eyes. Remember how you achieved your goal, solved a difficult life task, and learned something new. You did it, you did it! Keep moving; raise your hands up. What did you hear then, what did you feel when you were a winner? Your body must remember this. Now come up with some kind of gesture. Clutch your fist and say to yourself: "Yes! I am a winner! I can do it! It's cool; it's a life that is changing right now!" You can gradually slow down, exhale. Take a comfortable place.

We believe you continue to smile. You have just included moments of drive, movement, unrealistic annealing, a strong internal state. You combined your success story with new positive energy, created an anchor. Analyze your condition - how has it changed, what feelings and emotions have you experienced? How did this exercise go for you? How has your mood changed? What happened as a whole? Surely your mood has improved, there is a desire to do something. This suggests that the result is already there - increased energy, there was an internal impulse to activity. Moreover, in principle, right now you have not become someone else. You just performed a few actions that are available to you in everyday life.

This tool is very simple. With it, you can turn on your mood and any state that you need. The more unique the anchor, the better. We recommend that you put a strong anchor, that is, do not just scratch yourself. Squeeze your fist, squeeze it tighter and tighter - this is a strong anchor! This way you can turn on the peak state you need. Whether you will use the specific state that you have created now or some other, it does not matter - but you need it. You need a resource internal state, and remember that it can be different. When switching from ordinary to more active actions and results, the first thing you need is to create an internal peak state.

Exercise

Write three internal states and names for each of them. Literally, in two or three lines describe each. Choose the conditions that you will need for life. For example, high concentration, a state of the crazy drive, relaxation to exhale and slow down. This is an example. One of these conditions must necessarily be very strong, active, or very energetic.

Then, for each of these conditions, recall the situation that you will present. The most important thing is that you live in this situation, that you remember everything that you saw, heard, and felt then. You must close your eyes and imagine that you are there, to gain access to this condition. Next, you reinforce this situation with anchors. An exercise must be done for each of the three states, and for each of them, you need to come up with and write an anchor that you put on them. Anchors should be different, especially if the states are different in energy. For a calm state, one, for a drive one, is completely different. What is it for? Firstly, this is how you learn to turn on and control any state. If you control your inner states, you control emotions. If you control emotions, you will be able to control your actions. When you control actions, you control the results for which we, in fact, started the process of personal growth. It all starts with managing yourself! The control of internal states is the control of oneself. This is what the exercise we just completed is for.

Anchors - a technique that can be used in everyday affairs. You need to slow down - open your task, remember the situation, the music and do the exercise. This skill needs to be developed; it is necessary to get used to it.

Tasks

1. Write three internal conditions that you will use in life, at work, on vacation. Anything that can be useful to you. For example, "disco drive."

2. Give a name to each condition and describe it in a few sentences.

3. Remember the situation in your life when you already had the right condition. Connect with the experiences of the past: what you saw then, what you felt, heard ... Close your eyes and completely immerse yourself in that state.

4. When you get this state here and now - put an anchor on it (turn on the music, make characteristic movements).

Chapter 4

The Fourth Step:
Closer to the Body

Let's start with a little workout. Stand, straighten your back, shoulders, smile and start moving to the music. Shake yourself (especially if you are after a hard day's work), recharge your batteries for new knowledge and skills.

Let's repeat three key points, three main tools of your motivation.

1. Resource state caused by anchors. It can be a state of concentration, drive, relaxation.
2. Pain is a kind of shock, a painful effect on oneself and one's life.

3. Focus on the goal - the conclusion on the positive, on the drive, visualization, presentation of your future, a wonderful picture of your desired life.

So, these are the three key elements, and they are already working to incorporate motivation. You can recall your emotions for a short time - how you felt pain, drive, focused on goals, and went into a resource state. You managed to get involved in this process; it was not difficult. Now you not only know about this in theory, but also did it, felt it.

Unlimited Energy from Within You!

Now let's move on to the topic of motivation tools. We will analyze one of the tools of unlimited energy - your body. Let's talk about everything related to the body - physiology, nutrition, physical activity. In terms of the body, there are several tools - those that work for quick response, and those that contribute to the long-term inclusion of themselves. These tools are different, and they act differently. In life, you use both categories.

Remember how a couple of minutes ago you did a workout? What happens when you move from a tired and a bit lethargic state to an active one? You start the movement, change the facial expressions on your face, and smile. You do just a few simple things with your body and your energy level changes. For instant inclusion, this works very well. If you need to get involved before a speech or important talks, now you know what needs to be done. You have a resource state, and to go into it, you use your anchors. You straighten the body, shoulders, back, make several movements - and that's all. To get energy for a short period, do just that.

Exercise

How to include motivation for a long time, to constantly be in a good mood, in the right resource state, to have a bunch of energy and strength to achieve long-term goals? For energy to be with you for a long time, for you to feel good every day, you must complete the following task. The first is the morning block (or hour) of strength. This must be done every day! If you do, great. If not, then you need to start - to get energy and motivation. The morning hour of strength is a physical and emotional setting, recharging with energy so that the whole day goes positively. Firstly, when you wake up, your first thought should be sunny, major. What do people usually think? "Well, damn it, the weather is bad, it's cold, it's dragging to work now, also through all traffic jams. How awful it all got me!" This is a loser strategy, an example of how you don't need to think. Wake up in the morning, the first thought: "Cool!" Get used to saying yourself a positive word in the morning.

Try to do this even for no reason. If you have a reason, so much the better! If you still don't know what to enjoy, then still start smiling. After all, the first thought with which we wake up, the first morning minutes and hours set the mood for the whole day. A successful and positive person wakes up - he already turns it on automatically. Your task is to have positive and energy automatically turned on in the morning. What do I need to do? The first, as we have already said, is a positive thought in the morning. It doesn't matter what your period of life is. It doesn't matter what the weather is like - everything is cool! Even if you are in the pit, rejoice at least for the reason that it simply cannot be worse. This is already a good reason to smile. You understand that your affairs are so bad that it will not be worse. Therefore, tomorrow and the day after tomorrow will only get better. Transform any negative situation into a positive experience. If there are any problems in your life - this is experience, you learn something and become stronger.

Remember the task of pain. You immerse yourself in negativity, you are in pain, it is unpleasant, you do not want to live and work with all this. This is a huge force, tremendous energy in order to move on. Therefore, no matter what happens in your life, always try to include positive. Further, we pass to affirmations. Personally, I (Walter) do this: I wake up, immediately smile, and say something positive. Then I go to the window, look at the clouds, houses, trees and say: "Today is the best day in my life!" I pronounce this phrase loudly, fully living it. At this moment, the feeling comes that today is really the best day of my life. There are always a million reasons for this, you can't even explain them to yourself. Say affirmation in a tone that you yourself believe in it. If you pick up the wrong intonation, then this will not work. You turn on your resource state and already in it say that this is the best day in your life.

Next, in the morning you need to do a jog or exercise. We recommend jogging, as aerobic exercise and fresh air pump your breath and remove many clamps. Today, people have a lot of "clamps" in the chest, in emotions, breathing. Observing people, we very often see this. What happens to you with excitement or during a difficult situation? The first - breathing is lost, it becomes superficial and very shallow. Many people live with this all their lives. At the same time, when everything is fine with you, the chest is straightened. Breathing immediately becomes calm, deep.

It needs to be developed and running in the morning helps. It is not necessary to run a few kilometers, getting very tired at the same time. You need a morning run in order to recharge your batteries. If you run so much that you barely dragged your feet home, the day may go wrong. You will have to recover for two or three hours. Take a small but energetic run to avoid running out of breath. You can do it short and at a very calm pace. This will also help you achieve your goal - to turn on energy.

Be sure to drink a glass of clean water before jogging. Water has a positive effect on the body. Over the night, the body loses moisture, which must be replenished. Therefore - a glass of water, go over to the shower, again a glass of water, then breakfast. Sometimes we ask: what to do with a run in the winter? Dress warmer and still run. Of course, it would be nice to get used to this summer, but you need to run in any weather. If the weather is really bad, then make a short circle. Choose your standard circle, advanced and shortened. Standard run every day, advanced - if the weather is very good, shortened - if it is snow, sleet, rain. You also improve your immunity. We see many people who run in the rain and snow - in any weather. It is absolutely normal if this becomes your habit. Another hardening chip is to pour cold water in the morning. It also includes the body well. This, again, needs some getting used to. Do not immediately make ice water; for a start, it is enough to make a little colder than usual. So three days, then even colder, gradually lowering the temperature more and more. Accustom yourself in stages, so as not to immediately catch a cold. At the same time, carefully monitor the state of your body. Watering can be done optionally, that is, if you want to - pour it on, if you want - not. So far, this is not included in the main task. If you have not been involved in sports before, then you should not give a big load right away. Increasing it gradually is what works great for energizing.

Pay attention to your body - do you have muscle cramps, what is your posture, in what position do you walk, sit, sleep. What does a depressed, listless, lethargic person who has little energy look like? Most likely, he has stooped shoulders, his shoulders are lowered, his back is hunched over, his head is tilted down, and his gait is lethargic. A dull impression, isn't it? Now let's imagine how a person looks peppy, energetic, and self-confident. What is his body, gait, posture, face? Such a person, most likely, has a measured step, a smile on his face, a direct look, good posture. From today, starting right from this moment, pay attention to your body. Think about what type of people you want to relate to. Do you want to be the one who goes through life with a heavy burden, who does not succeed? Such a person has no motivation and energy; he is just tired of everything. Or do you want to be a winner? A confident person who looks positively at the world and achieves its goals? Such people have a high level of energy, confidence, self-esteem, they boldly go through life.

Control Your Body

Get used to keeping your back straight; shoulders should be straightened and relaxed. Do not forget about the smile and open gestures, do not cross your arms over your chest, do not tie your legs in a knot, do not slouch. Walk and sit straight - no need to tumble to one side. Imagine that a thread is attached to the top of your head that pulls upward to the clouds. Try to be in high condition as much as possible. If you are sitting, do not bend or slouch. Is your work monitor too low? Make a stand so that it is at eye level and you do not have to bend down to it. Just move the monitor higher; this will help keep your back straight.

Now I would like to talk about night sleep. Pay attention - how you go to bed, how you fall asleep, in what position you sleep. In the fetal position or in an open free pose on the back? Better to sleep on your back in an open pose. You may not believe this yet, but do an experiment. Compare your feelings - when you curl up in a knot and when you sleep openly. You will feel the difference. An open pose, as if broadcasts to the world that you are not afraid of anything. You are absolutely open and do not worry about what is happening. This is power! So try to sleep on your back. Start doing it today to fix the habit for the rest of your life. Falling asleep on your back will not work right away. When I got used to it, it was difficult for me too. Try to go to bed to think: "What a fellow I am, I fall asleep on my back, because I am confident in myself and my abilities. I sleep on my back, and this confirms my strength, my success."

An excellent option before bedtime to include music to which you have anchored a state of gratitude for everything done today. Associate falling asleep on your back with something important for yourself. There really is a direct connection - falling asleep on your back, you become a more relaxed person. Think about it; pay attention to it.

Relearning and Retraining

I am often asked if there is any methodology that helps retrain more effectively. Two answers can be given here. First, daily repetition is necessary. Secondly, connect with something significant, important for yourself with those actions that you perform.

Let's go back to the example with falling asleep. Every day, lie down and fall asleep on your back. If you suddenly wake up on your side

- roll back onto your back. Be sure to think about exactly how sleeping on your back helps you become successful. Some new things that you will get used to can be very tough and uncomfortable. It will be hard and uncomfortable. When you encounter such situations in your life, say to yourself: "Hurray! I have found a field for my growth!" Overcoming such situations, you grow as a person. If you are always comfortable, you are not developing. Personal growth occurs only through overcoming life's difficulties. This applies to all people. When you relearn, you have a new behavior, new habits. In this regard, the old become impossible for you, unimaginable. When a person truly quit smoking, it seems to him that cigarettes are a rare muck, which is even disgusting to hold in your hands. If you are used to sleeping on your back, then sleeping on your side is completely uncomfortable - it seems that your chest is pinched. Plus, you get better sleep on your back, and I confirm this fact.

Tasks

1. Include the morning block of power in your daily routine. Namely:

    ♦ do exercises (it is better to run in the morning);

    ♦ drink a glass of water on an empty stomach (buy good water);

    ♦ eat fruits or vegetables for breakfast (salads are available);

    ♦ do not forget about the positive attitude: "Today is the best day of my life!"

2. Add sports and physical activity to your life. Choose what you like best and do it daily or two to three times a week. It can be jogging, walking in the fresh air, swimming pool, yoga, gym and so on. In the report, write that you have chosen how often and at what time of the day you will do it. Excuses like "I have no time" are not accepted.

3. Pay attention to your body. Do you have muscle cramps? Is your back straight or are you slouching? What pose are you sleeping in?

From this day, control your body and get used to the following:

♦ straight back;

♦ the shoulders are straight;

♦ smile;

♦ gestures are open;

♦ sleep better on your back, open posture.

Chapter 5

The Fifth Step:
Perfect Day

Continuing to achieve our goals! How did you cope with previous exercises? What did you do and what didn't? Maybe everything was easy, or maybe the other way around? What seemed simple to you, what thoughts arose in your head during the exercise? We are very happy if it was easy for you and a lot of diverse thoughts arose. When you begin to be included in the creation of your future with a description of goals, then gradually thoughts begin to flow in a stream. Or maybe you were scared by the opportunity to dream, because writing about your future is not so easy, and you just can't imagine it? The problem is that we have only two options. First, we plan our future, and exactly what we want is happening in it. The second - everything is left to chance. This is exactly what happens in most people. All events occur suddenly; people just go with the flow. Since you decided to take this training, then this path is not for you.

During the exercises in this book, you gradually recall the goals and objectives, which can then be included in the plan. Often, plunging into the past reveals a lot of new and interesting things. And do not be afraid of the thought of how exactly you will achieve your plan. After all, subconsciously, you have long decided that you simply do not want to go with the flow. In fact, further on you will not be easy either. The exercises will be quite complex, but nonetheless will prove to be very valuable. Let's get down to one of them right now.

Please take paper and a pen. We will perform an exercise that will help you imagine the ideal future in which you will live. When you did the previous exercise, you might have a problem. It was quite difficult to imagine your future - what it looks like, what will be in it, what would you like to see in it. Or vice versa, everything turned out easily and naturally? If not, now we will begin to work with you on this.

The Perfect Goals

In order to truly achieve your goals, you need to imagine the perfect day you want to come to. Let's start presenting this perfect day. Quality of life has several key characteristics. We will ensure that we prescribe them, shaping your ideal life.

Imagine that some time has passed - a year, two, three. Let's say you have reached an ideal life. And the first thing I would like to talk about is your income, finances. Imagine your perfect day - how do you live? Where does the money come from? Maybe this is passive income - for example, from earned capital or investment. It is possible that this is the income from the business that you create. Or is it royalties from articles or books that you write? If you have plans to receive passive income, then write down right now where you will receive it.

At the same time, think and start writing what kind of active income you will have. Where will the money come from if, of course, in your ideal life you want to do something active that will bring you money? You might want to completely drop all work and live only on passive income, doing hobbies that you like, but do not make money. Many will want to continue active work, not to stop. If so, write down what sources of income exist in your ideal life. What do you do that brings you income? Maybe you work somewhere or engage in individual practice, advice, provide some services. Write what kind of activity you do to generate income.

Finance, Emotions, Joy

So, the first point is finance. Imagine what you do, how much time it takes, what money it brings, is your source of income constant or not. Go to the next item. The characteristics of life, which we will talk about later, are emotions. In fact, it is the salt of all life. This is the engine that will help you move forward. Imagine and write down how you will feel in an ideal life, what emotions you will experience during your ideal day. Describe only the highlights. Maybe it will be the joy and pleasure of each day spent. Or the joy of communicating with your loved one, children and friends. Or satisfaction from self-realization, vivacity, and tone from regular sports, an excellent mood with which you will wake up every morning. Perhaps you will describe harmony with the outside world, interest, and curiosity that will not fade in you until you are old. It is impossible to immediately imagine the whole variety of emotions that you would like to experience in your ideal life. But try to imagine the very cramps day you want to live. What emotions will it be filled with? Write them down, at least a few of the brightest and most colorful.

The next item is the skills and knowledge that you will have in your ideal life. The emphasis must be placed on skills, because knowledge, unfortunately, yields very few results. Surely you know a lot of smart people with a bunch of diplomas. Such people have read a huge number of books, but they are not representatives of a successful half of humanity. Therefore, skills are much more important - what you will be able to do. Think and write down what skills you have, which ones you have acquired, which, maybe, you are mastering now. Perhaps these are people management or sales skills if you are in business. This is one of the most important skills if you want to make big money. Or do you want to have the skill of public speaking or to be a leader and lead people? Maybe you want to become more charismatic and increase your inner strength.

If you want to transfer your knowledge to other people so that they can achieve success with your help, then perhaps these are the skills of mentoring, training people. Or do you describe some social skills? The choice is yours. Write out at least five of these skills, and preferably more. I do not know what exactly will be with you. Everyone has their own life, so everyone describes their own ideal day.

Next, I would like to talk about what brings you joy. Many do not pay attention to it, but it is very, very important. There are several types of satisfaction. The first is satisfaction from consumption. This is the lowest level: you get something, and you feel good about it. It is clear that such satisfaction does not last long. The second type - from the fact that something happened to you by itself. For example, you won a million dollars and are happy with it. The third type of satisfaction is that you set a goal for yourself, and then you hit it. Something happens to you, not by itself, but as a result of your own active actions. This is what you need to work on. There is another type of satisfaction. It is the joy of helping other people, making them happier. In this paragraph, we ask all of you to write down one phrase. It reads as follows: "Everything that I do brings me joy." We very much hope that you will agree with this statement and that it is really important for you.

Your Home Is Where?

The next item is the habitat. Re-imagine your perfect day, what it looks like. Describe where and how you live, what surrounds you. Do you live in the capital or in a small town? Or maybe you settled on the sea, in the mountains or in the forest? Whichever you like. It is possible that in the summer you live in one place, and in the winter in another. Look out the window for the weather. Is it raining there or is the sun shining? What do you see from the window of your house when you get up? How many rooms in your house or apartment, what do they look like? It is not necessary to record everything right now. Just imagine, take notes. Describe how the rooms are located. Is this a studio apartment? Two-story apartment? Own house? Many people aim to live in their own homes in nature. What furniture is in it? What kind of window opens? What is nearby - a pool, a swing, a playground? Imagine how far your home is from the city. From which city? In which country?

Record your ideal living environment. Do this in as much detail as possible, noting all the details that only you can imagine now. Maybe you live in several places - each for two to three months. Suppose you spend part of your time on a yacht somewhere in warm countries, and some more time in Iceland. Whoever likes it, there are no bad and good options. There is something that suits you; it seems to you that it is an ideal life.

Relationships

Next, let's talk about a category such as relationships with other people. How do you contact parents, children, a loved one, friends, neighbors in your ideal day? Maybe you dream of an ideal life with a loving and beloved family? Or do you represent many friends whom you regularly visit? Do you come and who comes to visit you? Also, note what your relationship with business partners is. How do you imagine interacting with relatives?

Do not describe your relationship with other people simply as "good." This is a very bad word because it is completely unclear what is meant. The more blurred the goals, the more difficult it is to achieve them. Therefore, we would recommend you write a little more in detail. Presenting your perfect day, pay attention to the various groups of people that surround you. Family, relatives, close relatives, friends, and colleagues - how do they feel about you? For example, imagine how your colleagues perceive you. Writing just "good" is like not writing anything. Do they treat you with respect and reverence? Do you know you as a strong, professional, and energetic person?

Health and Sports

The next item is health and sport. Imagine how you look, how you feel in your ideal life. We hope you write that you are healthy and feeling great. What does your body look like? How athletic and inflated are you? Are you flexible and energetic? What sports do you practice? How often do you spend time outdoors? You look at yourself in the mirror on your perfect day. What do you look like? Imagine a detailed picture. Try to briefly describe it in words. But it's much more important than you can imagine.

Little Time?

The next item is your time. Think about how and what you spend it on. If you have everything, but no time, then you can safely assume that you have nothing. Quite often, the following situation occurs. Surely you know people who do business, have a lot of money, but at the same time, they have absolutely no time. They simply cannot find a free hour or two to spend money or to enjoy other aspects of their life. We think this is not the best option for you and not at all what you want to come to in the end.

There are three key parameters in our world - time, money and mobility. This means the following: will you work today or not, with whom will you work, when and how will you work, in which place. A survey was conducted of businessmen, people who have achieved a lot. Only one question was asked: "What do you want to have more in your life?" Basically, everyone answered that they want to have more time. Imagine your perfect day again - how is it going? Think of a schedule - how your day goes, starting in the morning. When you wake up, what do you do in the morning, where and when do you go after breakfast, where do you work? Think about how much time it takes you on the road - or maybe you work at home? How do you spend your daytime? When do you do creativity or just your favorite thing? How much time do you spend on your own development (for example, reading books)? What are you doing in the evening? What social life do you lead? You should try to mentally live your ideal day - it is better to see the goal in the imagination than not to see it at all.

Money Difficulties - Business Applications for Setting Goals

The next item for those who are engaged in business. You need to figure out what you will do to ensure that the company works with your minimum participation. Imagine such a business. How does the system of attracting customers and sales work in it? How is the management of current activities? Who controls this business? Who protects it? How does money come to you? Business is a tool to achieve your goals. Remember, the business itself is not a goal but only a tool. Therefore, imagine this tool. Naturally, this will be a rough idea, but write it down, nonetheless. What kind of business will it be, what is produced in it, to whom and how is it sold, who runs it? Most likely, there is an executive director who manages current activities. You only control this process. If you are in business, be sure to do this part of the exercise to the end, it is very important.

"Value-Added Services"

Finally, we move on to the last point - what you bring to this world. What do you plan to leave after yourself? Please think: what is the cause that will live after you? Something that people will gratefully recall, realizing that this is the creation of your hands. How did you manage to present your ideal future? Did you like it? Did you manage to see more clearly the details that you previously had difficulty imagining? We hope so. Very often, we have the following thought in our head: "First, I will work forty-eight hours a day, and then, finally, I will begin to live the life that I dream of!" Have you ever had this? Have you ever said that now is not the time? "Then I will earn a lot of money, get a new job and then I'll start living the way I want!"

Unfortunately, "later" never comes. Often you set yourself a limit: business or family, health or money ... and so on. "Now I do life, then business." You must understand that all this must be done in parallel, move to all points, develop all the characteristics. This is a prerequisite; otherwise, you will not achieve anything and even lose health. Achieving goals on all fronts at the same time is possible, and this is what we should strive for.

Exercise

We pass to homework. It is not only for today but for the rest of your life. Every time you take up something, you must ask yourself questions: does this fit into your ideal lifestyle? Does this help to achieve a perfect day? Every day brings you closer to happiness. Yes, this is a small step, but it should help you get closer to the ideal day. At the same time, you should have time for family, leisure, sports, friends, and work - for everything that is important to you.

By the way, why do you often see the things that fortune-tellers predict? It just so happened that fortune-tellers believe. We don't know where it came from, but some people perceive the predicted as if it should certainly happen. We have already said that if you think about your goals and fix them on paper, they seem to be marked with red flags. You begin to reflect on these goals daily. And if a fortuneteller tells you something, her prediction crashes into your mind. And so further life happens in the way you guessed it. It really doesn't matter what you want. When you determine your goal, your life is built so that you come to it. Some things begin to change, and everything happens as you intended. Therefore, the predictions of fortune-tellers come true. But when other people predict your life, it is they who take responsibility for drawing a specific future for you. They just pick one of tomorrow's many options and show it to you. And you begin to move in a given direction. But, you yourself must be a predictor of your fate because everyone is endowed with such abilities. You just need to learn this skill so that you can build life as you wish. It is very important to understand that each of us builds his life and receives what he wants.

Many people aim at a car, apartment, jet ski, plane, or helicopter. But you have the power to set yourself much more ambitious goals (especially for men). A woman is able to realize herself in the family. If she has a good husband and children, then often this is enough for her. For a man, family alone is usually not enough. A man by his nature strives for achievements. He needs to realize his potential outside the family, and then he really feels the fullness of life. In this case, women love him much more, and, accordingly, everything he does is excellent. For both women and men, it is important to know what mission they carry. Sooner or later, we will come to realize what we really want in this life. Everyone has a global goal. Now is the time to determine what your mission is. This task will be quite difficult.

Imagine that many years have passed after your death, and now the journalist is creating the story of your life. He writes about what you have achieved. Try to describe as much as possible in the words of an imaginary journalist what you have achieved in your entire life. It is very important to pay attention to details. The tasks that you have already completed and the goals that you set will help you with this. Try to describe your life in as much detail as you can imagine. The task is not easy and will require about an hour and a half to complete. We ask you to set aside time for this and do it immediately when the opportunity arises. Try to make sure that no one bothers you while doing this exercise. Sit down and create your story, your obituary. Need to write in the past tense - was, had. For example: "He had so many plants, he had such a family." Describe where the person lived, how many floors were in his house or rooms in the apartment. How he spent his day, how he (it is very important!) Celebrated an anniversary of fifty or sixty years - depending on what date is important to you.

Try to write as detailed as possible, from today to the very end of your life. This exercise must be done when you are alone and can gather your thoughts. Here you can't get by with a few suggestions, at least you should get an A4 page. Very good if there will be more. I recommend writing by hand. And when you begin to layout your work as a report, you will print it and you can once again get in touch with the history of your life. This is the first task you need to complete. The second task in this training is constantly repeated every day: you take the next action from each area of your life (a list made at the very beginning) and perform this action tomorrow. The most important thing is to get the result. Your obituary is so far only drafts that will need to be finalized. You will return to it more than once to supplement it. This is because, in the process of your life, values will change, new ones will constantly appear. You just want more. Don't you think the composed obituary is unrealistic? We want to say whether the goals that need to be achieved do not seem unrealistic. Indeed, it will take a lot of work. If you want to achieve big goals, you must have a global dream. Not just buy a car or apartment, but, for example, help thousands and even millions of people. If you have a truly serious goal, you need to work hard, work on yourself.

When you detail goals and dreams, they take on a different meaning. When you clearly imagine the goal, then it is easy to move to it. So it turns out for those who have repeatedly worked on their goals. If there is no detail, the obituary needs to be further developed. Add more specifics. If you describe that you live in a house, then try to imagine what it looks like. How many floors are there, what are the rooms and which is your bedroom? Try to present the picture more clearly, in great detail. We advise you to read the obituaries of other participants in the training (if your friends are with you, or possibly your spouse). Sometimes you read, and the story told really sparks, and you are driven - "I want to act."

Working with goals, of course, requires a fairly long time. Sometimes, in order to achieve a certain goal, it is necessary to sacrifice something fleeting. This is necessary to understand what you really want, what goals are imaginary, and which are true. Someone couldn't write anything except the words: "I'm a modest person and I don't believe in the sincerity and truthfulness of obituaries." Regarding modesty, there is one interesting saying that I heard during a charm training. It was led by a woman who said such an amazing thing that I immediately wrote down on my notebook. She said: "You are either humble or happy." There is no third. And indeed, it is. The more modest you are, the less you achieve. The more you do, the more desires you have, the more chances there are to hurt someone and become someone unpleasant. This is because it's impossible to please everyone. You need to shove your modesty to hell and let your true "I" get out. You need to get to the bottom of what you really want to get in life. You should think globally, forgetting about modesty. As they say, modesty adorns, but everything should be in moderation.

Many are faced with the fact that writing your own obituary is somehow uncomfortable. This is due to unpleasant associations. It seems to be logically clear that there is nothing wrong with it, but it's still difficult. If this variation of this exercise does not suit you, try to change it a little. Imagine that you are ninety years old, you have lived a very interesting and fruitful life, and your grandchildren are asked to tell about its most significant moments. You tell about all your victories - in writing. You can perform the exercise in such a way that everything looks in a positive way. The essence remains the same: you imagine yourself, looking from the future on your way from the mountain that you have already climbed. You see how you overcome obstacles, how and what you achieved. If you succeeded in doing the exercise, it means that you were able to touch your depths, your fundamental values. Now your frame of reference is beginning to emerge, according to which you will evaluate everything else.

Keeping in your thoughts a clear image of what you want to achieve, you will always be aware of what you are doing, how your day will go. Some are trying to be effective. In fact, there is no point in doing this. Imagine that you are climbing the ladder of success, and at its very top you realize that it was mounted on the wrong wall. That is why we give such tasks where you need to spend time and write a lot. You need to perform them so that you decide on the deep values. Based on this, you should begin to build a model of the right life.

Tasks

1. Imagine your ideal day in the future (in two to three years or more). Describe the main areas of your life: sources of income, emotions, environment, skills, and knowledge, sports and health, relationships with others, time and daily routine, business, as well as what value you bring to the world.

2. Write your obituary. Imagine that many years have passed, and now you are a journalist who creates the story of your life. Try to describe in as much detail as possible everything that this person had, what he did, what kind of personality he was, what kind of relationship he built, and so on. Use the goals that were spelled out in previous assignments, and compose your life story.

3. Select one action from each category and do it tomorrow.

Chapter 6

The Sixth Step:
The Foundation of Life

We begin the sixth stage of our training. How are you doing with the mood? Did you manage to complete the exercises, what difficulties arose? Record all these points, they are important. Working with goals is quite difficult. When you just start doing this, a lot of things are not very easy and not everything works out. But as soon as you start practicing this constantly, then everything comes out much better. We are constantly working with our goals, and constantly new things appear that we want to see, which we want to develop. To give a concrete example: there are many people who spend time on having a large income, or they want to be very popular. When they achieve all this, they suddenly discover that when they achieved their goals, they lost something more. What really was important. And now this is forever lost. In a completely different way, the life of a person who clearly understands what he wants is taking shape. Try in the everyday hustle and bustle to imagine the world around us as a picture. For example, you just sit in a room in front of a computer - and this is the picture you presented.

First, look at yourself from a close range. Then begin to gradually move away the image - you imagine yourself, for example, from the tenth floor, then from the height of an airplane, and then from space in general. When a picture of the whole world opens before your eyes, the realization of the fuss of a person who just sits and performs some kind of action comes. What does this person do and how much does it really fit into his global goals? It is always necessary to imagine such a voluminous picture. When you see it, when you have a daily awareness of what comes from deep goals, then it becomes much easier to perform some kind of action. In this case, they will no longer contradict your deeper goals.

Earlier, you were given a task for the rest of your life. Now that you are going to take up some business or make a decision, go to the picture of your ideal day. It is also necessary to return to your obituary. Always ask yourself: "Does my decision match the picture that I painted for myself, which I'm going to?" Only then will you make truly balanced and competent decisions coming from the depths of your soul. They will be correct and will help you to achieve your goals with dignity. This must be recognized. If you have not completed this exercise, you will definitely need to do it. If you did it without revealing the details, you need to complete the exercise. Those who have done well enough can be left at that level. But still, after a week, a month, you need to return to the obituary and re-read it again. This will open up energy for you, help you return to your goals and gradually refine them.

Working out Your Own Self-Esteem Issues

I am often asked: I am battling with low self-esteem, how to maintain motivation? How to motivate yourself? Where to start?

Of course, a person's level of self-esteem directly affects his goals, although he does not always realize the relationship between self-esteem and his goals. The self-esteem of a person has several degrees. High- It manifests itself in the fact that a person is confident in himself, optimistic, positive about himself, others and his future. Low - Inherent in people who are characterized by anxiety, insecurity, a tendency to pessimism. Adequate - Inherent to people who really value their abilities. They build their life and professional plans taking into account real conditions and opportunities.

The type of self-esteem affects whether a person achieves his goals as a priority or whether he succumbs to the goals of other people and circumstances. If a person has low self-esteem, he underestimates his abilities and capabilities and, therefore, sets simpler or underestimated goals than those that he really can and can achieve. With low self-esteem, a person often shows conformism, adapts to circumstances and, pushing his own goals, fulfills the goals of other people. With excessive self-esteem, on the contrary, a person can overestimate his abilities and capabilities and strive to achieve unrealistic goals. If a person has adequate self-esteem, this contributes to his success. The trouble is that there are very few people with adequate self-esteem. Therefore, from the standpoint of achieving success and setting goals, it is better if a person has high self-esteem than an understated one.

Discussing the relationship between self-esteem and goal setting asks yourself the following questions. When planning your life and work, are you trying to develop your strengths or seek to compensate for the weaknesses? Do you criticize yourself more internally or praise more? Are you willing to start a new business? Are you very worried in front of a large audience? Do you consider yourself a capable person? If so, in which area? Do you think that compared to your peers (classmates or colleagues) you have achieved greater success than they are? Can you say about yourself that your life was a success? Take as an example: building a house. The process does not begin with the fact that you take boards and immediately begin to build. And from the fact that you mentally imagine what your house will look like, what you want to see in it. What will be the living room in it, what kind of bedroom, where will the bed be, how many guests can be accommodated, and so on. That is, before you start building, you will think over all the details in your head.

Then you draw projects, make drawings, sketches, and develop a construction strategy. The main thing is not to miss the slightest detail; otherwise, you will have to make costly changes. You will need to hire a person who will correct your mistakes. Work on goals just includes what you have drawn in your life's project — what you want to see in it. Take another example, this time from the business sector. Why do many businesses fail? Most likely, because when planning there was some kind of omission. A person could simply not take into account all the elements and subtleties of the market he enters.

When planning your business, you need to see everything: what products are in this market, what is its pricing policy, what would you like to get in the end? And only after a systematic and detailed study you need to begin to act. Most proceed immediately to actions and only then they try to correct all the shortcomings that had to be paid attention to initially. The same goes for parenting. Many see themselves as good parents, family people. If you want to see your children disciplined, responsible, then this must be remembered and used in communication with children. If you practice this practice daily, only then will it produce results.

If you are battling with low self-esteem, well, you know, from my own personal experience, I can say that a good way to increase self-esteem is to achieve a result. In any area in life. Though a little one. And then again. And further. And go on a broad road that will lead you to the treasured self-esteem. In general, however, the devil lies in the word itself. To increase self-esteem … you need to stop evaluating yourself.

Let us return to the model of setting and achieving goals. Gradually, we begin to clarify the situation. You should already see a global picture of what you want to achieve in life. Further, we will concretize so that from your sketch you get a certain map of life, along which you will move.

The "Life Map" Exercise

Now, you have a new assignment. It is for those who have already coped with the previous one. Those who did not do this need to complete their obituary and specify it. After that, you can start the task for today and tomorrow.

You need to make a Life Map - a map of your life. The X-axis shows your current age, and the Y-axis shows the areas of your life. It is necessary to arrange them as follows: family, health (sports can also be included here), personal growth, career, business, career, creativity, entertainment (or leisure). On the X-axis, indicate your age, and this is done as follows: if you are twenty now, the first period will be twenty-thirty years, the next thirty-fifty, then fifty-sixty and sixty-one hundred. You need to make your life map, starting from the age in which you are now. If you are twenty now, then those periods are given that are given as an example. If you are already thirty, forty or more, then, accordingly, you start with this figure.

Take your obituary, an ideal day assignment, and try to jot down goals in each of the columns of the realms of life. You will see how everything fits together. For example, if you want your first child to appear at thirty, you will notice how this combines with your health. So, a couple of years before this, you need to start preparing yourself to become a mom or dad. This will affect your business, career. How much you will have to earn by this moment, how this will affect the purchases you make. On the life map, you begin to link all the things that we talked about earlier into a single whole. You need to assemble a mechanism that will work synchronously, where the elements will not interfere with each other.

Take another example from the field of career and business. There is a certain person who is twenty years old. At thirty, he wants to become a management company. Accordingly, he needs, for example, five years to prepare in terms of personal growth. A person begins to prescribe his goals: to take a certain course, to learn English. And by the age of thirty, he, possessing the appropriate skills, will achieve his goal. All the goals that you set for yourself must be prescribed. So you will see how much each sphere depends on the other. Accordingly, you will need to draw up a certain plan. Goals need to be stated for the rest of your life. Those that you put on the first three to five years writing in more detail. You can highlight the details - what exactly do you want to do, what to achieve.

As for further goals, for starters, you can sketch them out schematically. Imagine how you will spend your free time, how it will affect your health, what income your business will bring. Think about what you will do at fifty, how to celebrate your anniversary. All this can be written in the entertainment section. If you planned to buy a car at some time, then you will already see what you need to do to get it. That is, your final point is buying a car. So, you will know what actions need to be performed at the preceding points. If you want, for example, to build several plants in sixty-seventy years, imagine how you will prepare for this. Consider what actions you will take to do this, what areas of life it will affect. All this must be taken into account and planned in advance so that at any moment, you can imagine where you are and how you are moving towards achieving your goals. You need to specify in more detail on your life map the path that you will follow. Why are we compiling this map? So, looking at it, you could draw exactly the path that you will take, proceeding from your life's deep goals. It is necessary to do this as clearly and concretely as possible.

Take the scope of business. For example, a person is twenty years old, and at thirty, he wants to earn a certain amount of money, for example, 100 thousand dollars a month. Accordingly, it is necessary to write on the life map the path in which he will go to this money. This is necessary so that you, starting today, clearly see the picture of what and when it comes to you. It should be not just like this: "Here I want to earn a million dollars!" This million is not supported by anything; you do not know how to earn it. And on the Life Map, you draw in detail the path that you need to go to your first million. There you can already more specifically see your goal. If it is not supported by any factors, then this is no longer the goal. It is not realistic, which means that it does not motivate you. We know people who say, "I want to be rich." But the goal, in this case, is completely incomprehensible.

Or another goal: "I want to have $ 100 million." Well, why do you need this money? You can't even imagine what you will spend it on. It is possible that in fact, you could have $ 2,000 a month to feel happy. You just need to look at your needs. Accordingly, on the Life Map, you need to register everything based on your long-term goals. The life map contains the path that you will take. Try to imagine what you will do in fifty to sixty years. This is the age when you may no longer be working or actively running a business. It is possible that you will be snowboarding somewhere in the mountains. You need to imagine how you will look at this age, what you will do. As for the family, describing their fifty-sixty years, many forget about their grandchildren. At this age, you will already have grandchildren, if of course, you want to have them. Think about how you would build a relationship with them. Look deeper, try to see the global picture of what you want to achieve in this life, what you want to have. The life map allows you to do this as detailed as possible. If we talk about the health sector, many do not prescribe how they will do it. You need to make it so that you can clearly see and understand how you will develop and maintain your health.

Many write: "I will be engaged in my health," but this is a very vague phrase. You need to understand what exactly you will do, what kind of sport to do. Remember what you wanted to do as a child, and make it your hobby now. Plan it on a life map.

Set Goals and Plan Actions Must Be Based on Age

For example: "At the age of twenty-seven, I start skiing" or "At the age of thirty-one, I begin to learn parachuting." I really liked one card where it was written that in thirty - thirty-five years a person is going to get married. He prescribed what he would do for this at the age of twenty - to get acquainted with the girls, take their phone number, and communicate daily. The goals in personal growth are set - to undergo training on seduction. The same thing in business is to increase the pressure on the business in order to earn more and have more free money. In this case, you can immediately see how everything is interconnected.

I would like to draw attention to various entertainments and travels. Unfortunately, many prescribe this category too generically. For example, you write that from thirty to fifty you will travel to the cities of the USA and to far abroad countries. Or you note that you will travel "abroad." Understand - this is fog, you yourself cannot imagine what you want. You need more specifics. Here is an example. In the field of entertainment and travel, one young man wrote: "Climb Mount Kilimanjaro, visit Thailand, go to the island of Bali." It immediately becomes clear what the person will do. Disclosed are certain goals that he wants to achieve. If you plunge into the field of travel and entertainment, I think each of you has dozens of things that you would like to do. Surely you dream of countries that you would like to visit. Plan it in your life - when exactly will you go, for example, to Bali. Imagine the age at which you visit New York and the age at which you visit Thailand. Try to plan your travels in detail. Of course, not everything will develop the way you want and plan. Life is very unstable, and no one is immune to change. But when there is a certain picture and there is a global vision, it becomes much easier to move along your path.

When I myself first drew this map, I noticed the following. Those things that I planned for twenty-six to twenty-seven years old now already exist in my life. In fact, when you have a clear goal, it's very easy for you to move towards it. The life map needs to be constantly improved; it needs to be specified because more and more new goals will appear in the process of your development. And then you will more clearly begin to plan everything.

Personal Growth

Now let's turn to the sphere of personal growth. Some make the following mistakes: you write a specific goal, for example, you are Spanish and you want to speak English fluently. And this goal is, for example, in the interval of thirty to forty years. This is generalized and incomprehensible. We can say with full confidence that spoken English is achievable in a year. In this case, it is not clear what exactly you are going to do from thirty to forty years. Studying an hour a day, you can learn English in just a year. Therefore, you can plan spoken English in the interval from thirty to thirty-one years. Next, you see that you have free time. Therefore, do not be afraid to go further - for example, start learning a new language. Accordingly, plan it on your life map, and then it will be more interesting.

A few words about the English language and the fact that it is quickly forgotten. This must be made a habit. For example, you have taught yourself to brush your teeth every day, the same with English. Constantly watch movies, videos, listen to audio, thus developing your language skills. If the usual A4 sheet is not enough for the card for you, then take a larger paper, draw on it. Many people create a map in a Microsoft Excel spreadsheet, which is also quite convenient. There you can take yourself as many places as you like and plan everything you want. So you don't have to make excuses for yourself (there is not enough space on the card, the pen does not write, the cartridge in the printer has run out) - just make this card.

Sometimes the question arises: how to plan your further development? How to dig deep enough to see what you will do, for example, at sixty or eighty? It is really very far away, and just making something up is not an option. That's why you and I composed our own obituary, performed the "perfect day" exercise. From these sources, you can draw ideas, choose the right moments. But do you even have to go far - plan your future for such a prospect? You decide it yourself. There are people who do not plan at all - neither their week nor even their day. You can plan nothing at all and live the way most live. I want to convey to you one idea: if you have a clear vision of what you want to achieve by the end of your life, it is much easier for you to move forward. In this case, you come to understand why you are doing daily work.

Charisma, Leadership, and Relationships

Now I offer a little touch on the topic of charisma, leadership, and relationships. The opposite sex is drawn to those people who have a goal. Women love precisely those men who have some purpose in life, who strive for something. Some people are asked: "What will you do tomorrow?" and they answer: "Yes, I don't know how I will live today, not to mention what will happen tomorrow or in a month ..."

What is the principle of choosing time intervals in the Life Map? First comes detailed detailing - plans for the year. Then follows a period of two years, five, ten years - here you will already write in less detail. The farther you look, the more difficult it is to see your future. However, some outline should be made.

Another task: choose the next action from the five that we prescribed in the first chapter and complete this action tomorrow. I wish you success in compiling your life map. Now you are already able to structure your life. You begin to come into contact with your goals, you see them more clearly. The energy that you have accumulated is not wasted. It goes on and on to help you achieve your goals.

Tasks

1. Make a Life Map.
2. Select one action from each category and do it tomorrow.

Chapter 7

Can't Do It
Handling Difficulty to Reach a
Goal or a Dream

We often hear all kinds of excuses as to why people do not achieve their goals. Moreover, many tread this path at the very beginning. He set goals, made a Life Map, wrote a plan ... and when it comes to daily work on his goals, then it all ends. Today I have a very interesting task for you. When participants do it at the training, "the head is immediately miraculously cleared." And all excuses disappear forever. Indeed, after this exercise, it's hard to say to yourself: "I will do it tomorrow." Did I intrigue you? Fine! Then read on - an interesting discovery awaits you.

There is a very good idea that the real motivation is one that inside, which advances, helps to overcome all obstacles. The "can't help but do it yourself" motivation is very effective, despite the negative in this phrase. Think for a second - the point is that you cannot do otherwise than take up this business and do it. This is a very strong motivation; it can be both negative and positive. For example, you cannot help but work because you don't have enough money and you will not be able to feed yourself. This is a matter of survival. Or: you cannot help but work because you insanely want to buy a new car. You cannot help but work because it is important for you; it is your goal. The strength of this motivation is precisely in the presence of a goal. There is an excellent exercise that will help you feel this condition. For its implementation, we will plunge with you into a primitive system, back to our roots. In those days, people still lived in caves; there was no Internet, phones, or other pleasures of life. Imagine yourself as such a person.

Close your eyes and start imagining. You are a primitive man living in a cave. You wake up early in the morning, it's damp and cool outside, and the cave is warm and cozy, a fire is burning. A spear and a bow are lying next to you, you are going to hunt, as it is necessary to feed your family. You leave the cave, meet one of your fellow tribesmen and go hunting together. Imagine - what does this person think about what? Does he think: "I would lie down now in front of the fire, yesterday I painted such a cave painting, I will love it" or "I will postpone the hunt for tomorrow"? Yes, what "tomorrow"?! If you don't go today, it's not a fact that you'll get anything at all! You can't postpone it in any way, because if you postpone it, you won't catch anything tomorrow, and the day after tomorrow it will be very hungry. The situation is very serious since it is about survival. You cannot help but hunt, because you cannot sit in a cave all day because of laziness. You go and get your own food. Imagine what this person is thinking. He goes hunting: "Now I will reach that forest like deer were there. If not, okay but I'll go home and drink beer." No, that's not what happens! A man walks and finds a deer. If he does not find today, then he will surely find tomorrow, because his prey is his life. Lazy? - Just die of hunger.

Now that you have introduced your ancestor, walked barefoot through the dew, went hunting, try to put modern thoughts into his head. It is about those thoughts that limit you. For example: "I will do it tomorrow." Imagine this thought occurred to this person. His reaction: "Brr! What tomorrow?! And if the rains charge? And if I don't find food within a week, the family will die and I myself will die." It is such a reaction that will follow if a primitive man puts in his head the thoughts that limit us today. Imagine that you from the future fell into the Stone Age. You see a man with a club who aims to kill a deer, and offers him: "Let's chat on social networks." The answer will be:

"What?! What social networks?! I'm trying to survive here, and you're talking about social networks!"

Did you manage to introduce yourself in the place of a primitive man? How does he react that answers to this? Have you managed to feel at least for some fraction the state of a person who cannot help but hunt, who simply has no choice? He was born at this time, in this cave, and he has no choice - he needs to survive. Maybe this person would like to climb a mountain and look at a wonderful sunrise, contemplating the light touch of the wind on the blades of grass. But he goes and hunts because for him, there simply are no other options. He cannot but hunt. Did you manage to feel this state? If you are a woman, then do the same. Imagine you are a Stone Age man. Indeed, in those days, fooling around was not an option. Thoughts worked in only one direction - to satisfy the need for food.

Another example of such motivation: the most motivated person is the one who wants to use the toilet. In such situations, there is simply no choice. To date, "I can't help but do it" is the following options: you have been fired from work, your money has run out, and whether you want it or not, you will stand up and go and earn it. Whether you like this job or not, whether you want to work on it or not, you go and work anyway. With positive motivation, the same thing happens. You fall in love with a goal so much, penetrate it to the marrow of bones that you simply cannot sit still. You start to move and questions arise: "How is this obtained? How can I make it better?"

Local results are secondary. If you have an intention to achieve your goal, get out of the hole, motivate with "I cannot help but do it." You will easily go through the difficulties that arise on the way. You will go through a routine, overcome tedious work because you will have energy. Your motto will now sound like this: "I cannot help but do it!" I want to do it! I am ready to do it every day for free! " This is a very powerful thing.

Exercise

Now we try to do the exercise. Repeat it later with a deep dive. Turn off all phones, the Internet, choose a time when no one will bother you. The first step of this methodology is to try on the role of a primitive man who hunts in order to feed his family. Now you tried to do it superficially, but in the future try to feel it deeper. Close your eyes, find the right music for yourself. Imagine a three-dimensional picture.

Imagine a cave: you go out with a club in your hands, it's hard for you. Feel as much as possible about this situation, as well as the state: "I can't help but hunt now, I have no other choice, I just go and do it." The condition must arise within you, and then try to anchor it. Next, throw a few of your typical excuses into the head of this person. For example: "I'll do it tomorrow" or "Well, first I'll play, and then I'll do it." You use these excuses every day; you definitely have them. You go hunting, and suddenly such a thought arises. What will happen, how do you react to this thought in a state of "I can't help but hunt"? See what happens. In this process, some of your installations excuses just fall off on their own. At the same time, the state "I can't help hunting" should be very strong. "I cannot but do it, I have no choice, I have to do it!" Create for yourself the peak state that we worked on earlier. Make this state as strong as possible, and then your favorite excuse will disappear before you have time to appear. New thoughts will appear in your head, and there will simply be no room for excuses. Next time, when excuse comes to mind, it will seem to you complete nonsense.

After you try on the role of a primitive man, feel a state of strong motivation, work in the same way with today's harmful thoughts. This will serve as a great workout for you. Tomorrow, try to live all day in a state of "I cannot do it." Waking up in the morning, traditionally start the day with an hour of strength, then jogging, shower, and breakfast. When going to work, remember the "I cannot help but do it" state and turn on your anchor for this mood. Try to stay in strong motivation for as long as possible, ideally - all day. In the report, focus on the description of the two main points. First: how easy was the exercise? How did your thoughts transform into the primitive environment? Second: did you manage to stay in a state of "cannot help but do" motivation all day? What emotions and impressions did you experience with this? How did it work in general?

As for later life, including different anchors, be it music or bodily signals. Add to this the state of primitive man. The more often you repeat these exercises, the longer you will be able to stay in a state of a high degree of motivation, the faster you will get used to living differently. Also, it will allow you to experience vivid sensations, get a completely new life experience.

Getting Rid of Harmful Habits

Everything that you do and think about forms your patterns of behavior, which are popularly called habits. The more often you do something and repeat something, the stronger it is fixed in your head. If you spend every day on social networks, it just becomes a habit. Even if you don't really want to go into this social network, you still automatically turn on the computer and type in the name of your favorite site. This must be fought! When you embed new habits, new patterns of behavior, at the very beginning, the neural connections of these new habits are much weaker. It is because of this that a new habit must be repeated. If you started running in the morning, then you need to run every day at least for a month. Only in this case, the neural bundle "I wake up and go running" will be fixed in your head. Whatever the weather, whatever the mood, you wake up and still go running. The same principle must be used when working with motivation. Sometimes we are asked: how often do we need to reinforce the anchors? You need to reinforce them every time you use them. As soon as you turn on the anchor, disperse this state, fix it one to three times. Sometimes this situation happens: "I ran a couple of times for more than a year, and then threw it away for several years. Where is the neural memory?" There is no guarantee that any good or bad habit will last a lifetime. Our brain is very cleverly designed, and there may be a lot of reasons why you stopped running and did not return to it for a long time.

The main reason for the constant runs was motivation and a growing habit. And then the motivation disappeared plus coincided with some event, for example, with a disease for a week. I didn't run for seven days, and it's good - I woke up in the morning, lay down - and I don't have to run anywhere. Plus, winter was cold on the street. Everything, the motivation is gone. A new habit is replacing - not to run in the mornings. This is how it works. In order to maintain habits, you must constantly perform certain actions. Remember this situation with neural memory: if you don't run for a month, then it's harder to start. Because another habit has already taken hold - do not run in the mornings.

There is another frequently asked question: can it turn out that the fastening will gradually turn out to be the anchor itself? He squeezed his hand into a fist - got a state, squeezed harder - clenched the anchor harder, and now, to fix it, you need to clench your fist even harder. When you clench your fist - you anchor some state, compress it again - strengthen the anchor. The more forces you exert, the stronger the anchor. Therefore - this is the same anchor that you just strengthened.

How to PUMP a Weak Link in a Motivation Strategy?

If you see that you do not have enough of an element to achieve the goal that it sagged, you need to strengthen it. For example, you feel that you could not connect to the target. At the same time, you understand that you want to achieve this goal, but did not connect with it. In this case, your task is to find options for fixing this error. This is related to the actions that we perform in the outside world. Sometimes, to turn on, it is necessary to intensify the pain. How can I do that? You can quit work, but it will be a tough option, or you can just piss yourself off. Wrap up thoughts that everything is wrong in this world, that everything is too complicated, and you will get angry. No need to drive yourself into depression. You just need to get angry and it will serve as a motive to change something in your life. You get angry and go do something.

Tasks

1. Try on the role of a primitive man who goes hunting for a deer to feed a family that "cannot help but hunt". Try to settle in your head his thoughts of today that limit you (for example, "I'll work tomorrow"). See what happens.

2. After you have been in the "primitive loafers," write down all your thoughts, feelings, and discoveries.

3. Live one day at work using the internal "I can't help but do it" condition and write down what you got: how your attitude to work, mood and effectiveness have changed.

Chapter **8**

The Seventh Step
Elemental Action

If you have not completed your life map, then you need to finish it before moving on. Long-term planning is the foundation of your whole life, so this task must be taken very seriously. Modify the Life Map, bringing as much detail and specificity as possible.

Now, let's do another very serious exercise. To do this, you need a pencil or pen, a piece of paper, a ruler and a compass. Take a blank sheet and draw the Y-axis and the X-axis on it. Then, draw a scale from 10 to 1 on the Y-axis. The highest point is 10, the lowest is 0, or a reference point.

On the X-axis, you post eight approximately equal lengths. Each one is a sphere of your life. For example, the first area is health. You need to mark on a ten-point scale where you are in this area. How do you feel, are you satisfied with your body, how are you doing with energy? Think and mark on this scale what level your health is at. Try to be as honest as possible. The next area is friends, which you also rate on a ten-point scale. How many friends do you have, do you keep in touch with them? If you have many friends and you constantly communicate with them, then put 10. The next area is personal life. Rate it too. The next area of life is career or business. Career - if you work for someone, business - if you have your own business. It's the same here - evaluate where you are. Put the mark that you consider objective. The next ones are finances. Evaluate how you feel financially. Are you satisfied with your financial situation today? How do you feel? Or maybe you need twice as much money? Next are spirituality and creativity. How are you developing in these areas? For everyone, this is their own: for some, it is drawing, for some, it is singing, but for someone it is religion. The seventh sphere is personal growth. Put the mark that corresponds to its level. The last area is the brightness of life. How intense are you spending your time? Each, again, will have his own way. Someone has the brightness of life associated with getting adrenaline, someone with a relationship, someone with travel. How do you assess the brightness of your life, what is it equal to on a ten-point scale?

Now, put the sheet with the resulting picture aside and take another one. Using a compass, draw a circle. Next, divide it into eight spheres - you get the so-called wheel of life. Eight areas are the same: health, friends, personal life, career or business, finance, spirituality and creativity, personal growth, the brightness of life. Now, back to the marks on a ten-point scale of each of the spheres. Transfer them to your wheel of life. You need to do this as follows: mark with certain segments, and paint over what remains inside. So, do with each mark. You should get a circle from the segments-spheres that you painted over. See how smooth it is. Pay attention to the areas in which dips have formed. In general, the wheel shows how harmoniously you are developing. If you see failures - this is just what prevents you from moving forward in other areas of life. Take, for example, a businessman. He is at work twenty-four hours a day; his business is in excellent condition. As a person, he makes a lot of money, earns an excellent income, and there are no problems with finances. But if he is constantly immersed in these two areas, then, most likely, his personal life fails, health deteriorates, friends leave. Spending all the time to one thing, you lose in the other.

If you feel that your business has stopped, then it's time to take a look at what area falls out. It is lagging areas that impede development and prevent normal progress. If your health is lagging behind, then it is completely clear that you will not have the strength to stand up and do some business. Therefore, it is necessary to tighten health. If your personal relationships are lagging behind, this also greatly affects your career or business. Pay attention to which areas you are most lagging behind. These are weights tied to your arms and legs. They do not allow you to move normally. All areas are closely interconnected and have an impact on each other.

Ideally, you should aim at around 10 in all categories. Your life, your happiness, depends on how successful you are in all these areas. It is very difficult to roll an uneven wheel. If the wheel is smooth enough, then it will roll without problems. Then it remains only to develop it even more. If you have failures, most of your energy goes there. For further work with the wheel, it is necessary to write out goals for two months in it from the life map. You take today or tomorrow, count exactly two months, and in each sphere of the wheel, note the goals that you want to achieve during this period.

For example, if we talk about the brightness of life - what would you like to accomplish in these two months? Maybe you dream of going on a vacation or visiting some interesting places? Write in the category of brightness of life what exactly you want to see in this area in two months. We turn to the field of health. What kind of person do you see yourself in two months? How do you want to feel? Accordingly, you need to prescribe the actions that you will perform. Running, exercising, going to the gym and so on.

If we are talking about the sphere of personal growth, imagine, again, what kind of person you want to see yourself in two months. How will you look, how will you talk, how to communicate with people, and what skills do you want to develop in yourself? Write down specific goals in the category of personal growth. You may need to attend certain training to develop certain skills. What courses do you need to take in order to speak English more freely in two months? Now, as you understand, we are starting to narrow your vision a little. We begin to more specifically prescribe actions, by performing which, you will unwind your life and make it rotate the way you want it to. Pay maximum attention to the lagging areas of your life. The first thing to do is to start developing them.

Tasks

1. Modify the Life Map.
2. Draw the wheel of life for the next two months.
3. Select one action from each category and complete it tomorrow.

Chapter 9

Step by Step to the Goal

Now that you have a complete understanding of setting and achieving anything and everything you want. For these purposes, the wheel of life and the map of life are ready. It's time to start embodying the plan. We hope that while reading this book, you have an irresistible desire to act, and you have already done a lot to bring your goals closer. It is perfect! It's time to get even more involved in the daily planned work to achieve your goals.

Parallel Planning

You have already begun to act, and now in parallel, you need to write a work plan. Parallel planning is that you are doing one activity and planning another at the same time. To get started, write a list of all the cases for one of your projects. Take the one that is given to you with difficulty. In the list, indicate the most important thing - where to call, what to write, whom to say. It is not necessary to sort the list right away; you will turn it into a clear plan later.

So, the first task: to create the structure of your project. Before you take it, take a preparatory step - brainstorm. Use the Mind Map, sheets of paper, or a whiteboard to do this. This is necessary in order to sketch out the structure of the project, think over the logical connectives of the blocks, write down all (even the craziest) ideas. All thoughts that are in your head need to be moved here. At this point, your plan will be as flexible as possible. In fact, this is not even a plan, but sketches for it: you transfer everything that is in your head to paper. This is a very exciting and creative process. For example, I brainstorm before the start of each project. I have a large magnetic whiteboard, half the wall. On it, I sketch all my thoughts about the upcoming activities. If you do not have such a board, sheets of paper will do.

When you transferred all your thoughts and ideas from your head to a paper or a board, make a to-do list for the project. The next step is to divide the upcoming actions into phases. See what tasks you need to do now, which you can delay until a little later, which are important, which are not very. It is necessary to divide the list into at least three to five stages, and then make a clear plan out of it. If you carefully look and analyze your successful projects, you will find that the structure is present everywhere. It doesn't matter what you did at the beginning but at the end. A project plan, divided into at least three stages, is already a structure. When you have all your affairs divided into at least three heaps, then at every moment of time, you are doing what you need to do right now, and you aren't grabbing for what needs to be done at the very end. Thus, you maintain maximum efficiency during the implementation of the project.

In the third step, I suggest you draw a mind map plan in the MindManager program. For me, this is the main working tool. A sufficiently complex and voluminous project (for example, training) makes it necessary to take into account very many details. In this program, it's very convenient to work out every little thing. What is this? These are the so-called mind cards or smart cards. MindManager allows you to depict any project in the form of a tree - there is a topic, subsections depart from it in the form of branches, from which sub-items branch. You can also write text there. Those who switch to MindManager in the future simply do not understand how projects could be done without this program. For example, in Word, doing this is very inconvenient after you have tried MindManager. This is an ultra-efficient tool for structuring any project.

Implementation

As soon as you have at least part of the plan for the upcoming work - proceed with implementation. When you plan and write actions to be completed, you do not need to try to create a plan for the entire project at once. If the project is large, if it takes more than one day, then it is not worth prescribing everything at once. Plan in detail only what you plan to do during the week. If you know what needs to be done, then plan; if not, then you can figure it out later. Everything else goes on a draft list. A plan for at least a week should be detailed. It is necessary to register by the day - what exactly will you do, at what time. At the start, you do not need to know exactly what and how you will do in the third or fourth stage. How you will complete your project - it does not matter so far, for starters you need to turn on, accelerate and enter the stream. If the project is large enough and long enough, if it is still not quite clear, then by default you cannot know everything. So, plan, do again, and plan again. Get started, even if you have only three points in the plan. This is enough to get started. For a quick start, it's even better when your plan is small and simple. There are three to five (maximum ten) points - that's it, let's go!

Allocate at least half an hour each day to plan the next steps. This time will be enough for you to outline a work plan for tomorrow. The principle of gradual movement must be observed: every day is a small step. No need to try to do everything right away, so as not to only instantly exhaust all your energy. Every day, take a small but clear and understandable step. You do it, introduce something new, and everything turns out. If you can plan more than a day, be sure to detail your plan. But do not force yourself unless you understand something in detail.

Benefits of Concurrent Planning

1. You have not yet completed planning, are already acting. One of the key problems with putting things off for later is that many get stuck at the preparation stage. When I had not yet used the parallel planning technique, I thought that you must first write a complete plan in order to clearly and accurately understand all the steps. Very quickly, my mind map turned into an unrealistically huge tree with a bunch of branches and a million details. A super plan is actually harmful; it deprives energy and motivation. When you see a huge mountain and do not understand where to start, then you very quickly drop the case. Therefore, start acting without completing planning.

2. You bring into the plan only what is really necessary now, and not some theoretically necessary things. When I analyzed my plans, I noticed that there are too many tasks in them, which ultimately turned out to be completely unnecessary. When your plan is flexible and you work with it, while implementing something, it remains relevant. You are bringing in what is needed right now.

3. Your plan is always relevant; as you create it, take into account the current situation. A lot is changing; new ideas are coming. A flexible plan is the right one. Parallel planning drives!

Milestones

The next task is to work with milestones. A milestone is an intermediate goal, a milestone in your project. Plan three to four intermediate goals for your project-specific and measurable. Their description should be as specific as possible. How exactly do you know that you have reached your goal? Example: three paragraphs of the report are written that can be handed over to the head. This is a very understandable goal; it can be verified and it can be shown to another person who will see the result and say that the goal has been achieved.

A good milestone marks the end of a certain phase of your project. At the end of each stage, you should have such a goal. For example, you create an info-business, you need to make a website for this, record some product. A ready-made website, for example, on which there is a subscription form, is a specific goal that you can see. Create such a milestone so that they logically complete the stages of work. An example of an incorrect milestone: write 1000 characters for a report. It is concrete, measurable, it can even be checked, but this is not a stage, not a finished piece of work. The correct milestone is given above - three paragraphs of the report are written that can be handed over to the head. This is a finished piece of work. An even better milestone is a written draft training program. This is a finished, concrete, logically completed stage. Be sure to use such a milestone; according to them, it will be very simple and quick to determine whether you have reached the goal or not. Now that you have a plan and milestone, you are acting. The time has come to somehow control this whole thing. The next task is control and monitoring.

Control and Monitoring

At least once a day, check your plan, mark the items completed. Immediately make all necessary adjustments to the plan, do not accumulate anything. The key to effective control and monitoring is regularity and consistency. You must always check your plan. One has only to postpone and check the plan, for example, once every three days, as it turns out that you forgot something, did not achieve something. When you regularly review and control everything, you maintain the optimal rhythm of work that you set for yourself. For effective control and monitoring, it is important to praise and reward yourself for successfully fulfilling plan items, as well as fine for failure to comply. However, focus more on rewards. Make a list of awards, small, large, all sorts of different from which you will encourage yourself. It may be something simple - drink juice, go to the movies.

Do not forget to praise yourself - no matter how strange and childish it sounds, it really works. As soon as you start praising and encouraging yourself, something inside of you turns on. It becomes easier for you to carry out the following stages and tasks of the project, increasing motivation for further activities. The more you file and fine yourself, blame and rebuke yourself, the less motivation you have. There is no desire at all to do all this. You did not fulfill one point, you punished yourself, the next day you wake up, and the inner voice says: "Well, to hell with it!"

Pay attention to children. When children are rewarded for something, they seem to glow. And next time they will continue to do this and will perform even better. And when the child is punished, he simply stops trying. Therefore, focus on rewards and more rewards. If you have not reached your goal, try changing the scope. You planned to earn at some point 5,000 dollars, but earned 500? Think that 500 is better than nothing. Analyze: what you did well and what could have been done even better. Work on the mistakes and at the same time, do not forget to praise yourself for the fact that to some extent you still managed to achieve the goal. Maybe not as I wanted, well, okay, next time it will turn out better!

Do not proceed to the next tasks until you complete all the previous ones. If you do not have MindManager, plan on paper or whatever you like. No need to bother with the absence of any program. If something is not there, do it differently. Do not stop yourself with such trifles. Get used to act quickly and implement all the information received at once.

Chapter **10**

The Final Tasks

You have already begun to act and are now writing a work plan in parallel. First, make a list of all tasks for the working draft. This is a draft.

The Structure of the Working Draft

1.) Use the MindManager, sheets of paper or a whiteboard to draw the structure of the project, think over the logical connectives of the blocks. At this point, your plan is as flexible as possible. This is a creative and exciting process!

2.) Break all cases from the list into project stages. This is your rough plan. The structure decides a lot, even if you work well in chaos.

3.) Draw a mind map.

As soon as you have at least part of the work plan, proceed with the implementation.

1.) Plan in detail only what you will do during the week, everything else - in a draft list. At the start, it is not necessary to know exactly how and what exactly you will do in the third or fourth stage. Everything can change a hundred times. Get started, even if you have only three points in the plan (and this is just good).

2.) Spend half an hour during the day to plan the next steps. This time will be enough for you to outline a work plan at least the next day.

3.) Work with milestones. Plan and write down three to four interim goals of your project-specific and measurable. The description should be as specific as possible. How exactly do you know that you have achieved these goals? Create these milestones so that they are the logical stages of work. Example: three paragraphs of the report are written that can be handed over to the head.

4.) Control and monitoring. At least once a day, check your plan, mark the completed items. If there are corrections - immediately make them to the plan, do not accumulate anything. Praise and reward yourself for successfully fulfilling plan points and fine for failed ones. Focus on rewards.

When you complete a task in this chapter, proceed to the next. Do not go further until you have done everything! Act quickly and implement the information immediately!

Conclusion

I want to congratulate you - you have read this book to the end. Step by step, you were led to the creation of an inexhaustible source of energy in the form of goals and their correct achievement. I hope that you liked the training and you will apply the acquired knowledge and skills in life. Perhaps you are teaching someone else.

Finally, I have a few recommendations for you. The first concerns issues. Most people run away from them, make their life problems less. If we take the business, the owner thinks: when will the day come, when the business will work without me, and I will lie on the beach without thinking about anything? If we talk about work, then most people dream of quietly leaving work at six in the evening and lie down on the couch at home. People seek a quiet life, strive to ensure that it is measured. If for your purposes you strive for such a life, then this is bad. You should have a different approach. When you see a goal in front of you, you must understand that the only way to achieve it is through problems. The more serious your goal, the more serious the problems will be on the way to achieving it.

You definitely need to change - transform your habits, attitude to certain things, worldview. And we change only by overcoming problems. If you set a goal, then immediately think about what problems you need to overcome in order to get qualities that can help achieve the goal. I repeat - most people run away from problems. They are ready to minimize their number in their lives. Your task is to do the opposite. Come up with problems. They will help you become a person capable of achieving your goals.

The second recommendation concerns chaotic movements. A spontaneous action model, when you rush like a tsunami, do everything at once and in all directions. For many people, it's always possible to act consistently in everything:

now this, then this, tomorrow, and so on. Such a model is bad for those who want to achieve something - people who are eager to achieve more in their lives. You never have enough time to implement everything in sequence. Therefore, it is necessary to run processes in parallel in order to do everything at the same time. Sometimes letters come to me in the style of: "I want to start my own business. What should I do? Should I launch my site? Should I launch a subscription system?" The right decision is to do everything at once.

Now you have learned to set goals, take energy from them - so that they nourish you, help you concentrate. You have energy, you have been given goals, and then this energy needs to be launched in the right direction. This is necessary to spend it competently every day, not to waste it. Most people have colossal amounts of energy spend on completely useless things. If you take the average employee, then out of eight hours he spends only an hour and a half on really necessary and high-quality work. All the rest of the time is wasted.

In this training, you learned the opposite. You can do as much in a week as you did in a month. Extract hidden reserves of your own effectiveness. You will be interested: "How did I crawl before, like a turtle, why did I slow down so much?!" This training accelerates. Gradually, you are polished to such an extent that it begins to give just a tremendous boost! You begin to introduce a spontaneous action model in your life. The most important thing is that everything superfluous is immediately cut off. You simply don't have time for unimportant and insignificant things, and they are automatically thrown out of your life.

Another key thing that I want to tell you about in the end is the correct answer to the question "What to do?" This question arises quite often. They ask me at seminars in the form of letters. "I want to achieve the goal. What should I do?" The correct answer is to take and do. You begin to act, to do at least something in the direction of your goal - do not stop! Even if it is the wrong course. But you get feedback; you can correct it. You introduce something into your life; you are looking for a new one, get acquainted. Therefore, if you are in doubt whether to do one or the other, start doing at least something! Any action is better than inaction.

The next, very important thing - a new one is necessary. The more you add new things — new places, new people, new business — the more powerful you become. Look at people: they try to do the same things, go to the same places, communicate with the same people, work at the same job, changing it occasionally. If something changes in their life, it's just something similar. This is suitable for most people, but not for you. You need to add as much as possible to your life. And if you have a choice: for example, to go to an old place or to a new one, always choose a new one. This will give you additional energy, knowledge, dating, a new vision of the world - that makes you stronger.

In conclusion, I will talk about one equally important idea. In the first half of life, we are looking for our own path, and the second path leads us. Therefore, you need to work on your goals. What you did during the training is only a part. Such work should be carried out regularly. At least once a year it is necessary to revise large goals and about once a month or two - small ones. Goals are changing; they need to be constantly adjusted and refined. One of the key tasks is to cut off excess knowledge, extra people and projects that you have outgrown. You must be able to remove from your life. In order for you to have something new, you need to get rid of the old, otherwise for the new in your life there simply will not be a place.

I congratulate you on the work done! I am very glad that you took it so seriously. You have achieved a lot in such a short time, and I hope that you will continue to realize yourself. Deepen your knowledge, develop skills, and use them to achieve your goals. I have no doubt that you will definitely come to your plan!